A Month of Prayer with

St. Catherine of Siena

Wyatt North
BOOKS THAT INSPIRE

A MONTH OF PRAYER WITH ST. CATHERINE OF SIENA

Saint Catherine of Siena was born during an outbreak of the Plague in Siena in 1347. She was brought up in the faith, and especially after her sister died at the age of sixteen, found herself committed to pursuits of piety. She joined the Dominican Order and, at twenty-one years old, had what she described as her "mystical marriage" to Christ. Today, we know St. Catherine mostly through the many letters she wrote to her fellow brothers and sisters in the faith, and through a collection of visions recorded largely by her fellow nuns as she grew close to death. These meditations combine her letters with several of these revelations wherein she speaks in the first person as though speaking from God himself. In her letters and meditations, she speaks at great length about obedience, the centrality of Christ crucified to the faith, and how virtue should be pursued in our quest to grow in intimacy toward God.

INTRODUCTION

St. Catherine urges us in today's meditation to exercise moderation in all things—most of all, in the manner we love. To love earthly things excessively becomes idolatry. To love God exorbitantly without a love for our fellow humans is not a love of God at all. To love moderately is to love all things in their proper portions, with an appropriate devotion.

Day 1

Meditations from St. Catherine

I Catherine, thy poor unworthy mother, want thee to attain that perfection for which God has chosen thee. It seems to me that one wishing so to attain should walk with and not without moderation. And yet every work of ours ought to be done both without and with moderation: it befits us to love God without moderation, putting to that love neither limit nor measure nor rule, but loving Him immeasurably. And if thou wish to reach the perfection of love, it befits thee to set thy life in order. Let thy first rule be to flee the conversation of every human being, in so far as it is simply conversation, except as deeds of charity may demand; but to love people very much, and talk with few of them. And know how to talk in moderation even with those whom thou lovest with spiritual love; reflect that if thou didst not do this, thou wouldst place a limit before perceiving it to that limitless love which thou oughtest to bear to God, by placing the finite creature between you: for the love which thou shouldst place in God thou wouldst place in the creature, loving it without moderation; and this would hinder thy perfection. Therefore thou shouldst love it spiritually, in a disciplined way.

Letter to Monna Alessa Dei Saracinia

Additional Biblical Reflections: Ecclesiastes 3:1-8; 1 Corinthians 6:22; Philippians 4:8.

PRAYER

Dearest Lord, you have called us to love you with all our heart, soul, and strength. Yet, in the very next breath, you've bid us to love our neighbors as ourselves. Give us love in its proper proportions: wholly devoted to you and likewise to our neighbor. Amen.

DAY 2

In today's meditation, St. Catherine reminds us that our spiritual growth comes in its proper order. One does not become a saint without first exercising the foundational virtues of love and piety. One does not love one's neighbor and, thereafter, discover the truth, but one sees God's truth when living a life bathed in divine love.

MEDITATIONS FROM ST. CATHERINE

The soul, who is lifted by a very great and yearning desire for the honor of God and the salvation of souls, begins by exercising herself, for a certain space of time, in the ordinary virtues, remaining in the cell of self-knowledge, in order to know better the goodness of God towards her. This she does because knowledge must precede love, and only when she has attained love, can she strive to follow and to clothe herself with the truth. But, in no way, does the creature receive such a taste of the truth, or so brilliant a light therefrom, as by means of humble and continuous prayer, founded on knowledge of herself and of God; because prayer, exercising her in the above way, unites with God the soul that follows the footprints of Christ Crucified, and thus, by desire and affection, and union of love, makes her another Himself. Christ would seem to have meant this, when He said: To him who will love Me and will observe My commandment, will I manifest Myself; and he shall be one thing with Me and

I with him. In several places we find similar words, by which we can see that it is, indeed, through the effect of love, that the soul becomes another Himself.

A Treatise of Divine Providence

Additional Biblical Reflections: Psalm 119:97; Romans 13:8-10; John 14:21.

PRAYER

Lord, you have set forth a path toward you that follows from love and virtue. Lead us in the basic virtues that through the practice of such piety, we might grow, as a babe on milk before moving onto solid food, and reach full maturity in our devotion to you. Amen.

DAY 3

The life of a disciple is not one of comfort and ease. Christianity is not a feel-good religion. We have a God whose heart aches for the lost, for sinners, and suffering. A love reflecting God's heart will likewise ache. However, these pains are not without their use. In pain, we learn patience, and through patience, we come to know the truth and peace that comes through God's presence.

MEDITATIONS FROM ST. CATHERINE

Very pleasing to Me, dearest daughter, is the willing desire to bear every pain and fatigue, even unto death, for the salvation of souls, for the more the soul endures, the more she shows that she loves Me; loving Me she comes to know more of My truth, and the more she knows, the more pain and intolerable grief she feels at the offenses committed against Me. You asked Me to sustain you, and to punish the faults of others in you, and you did not remark that you were really asking for love, light, and knowledge of the truth, since I have already told you that, by the increase of love, grows grief and pain, wherefore he that grows in love grows in grief. Therefore, I say to you all, that you should ask, and it will be given you, for I deny nothing to him who asks of Me in truth. Consider that the love of divine charity is so closely joined in the soul with perfect patience, that neither can leave the soul without the other. For this reason (if the soul elect to love Me) she should elect to endure pains for Me in whatever mode or circumstance I may send them to her. Patience cannot be proved in any other way than by suffering, and patience is united with love as has been said. Therefore bear yourselves with manly courage, for, unless you do so, you will not prove yourselves to be spouses of My Truth, and faithful children, nor of the company of those who relish the taste of My honor, and the salvation of souls.

A Treatise of Divine Providence

Additional Biblical Reflections: Psalm 37:7-9; Luke 8:15; Romans 12:12; 2 Peter 3:9.

PRAYER

Lord, in great patience, you endure our faithlessness so that we might be preserved until life in your name. Grant us patience as we endure sorrow in the world. Let us ever be mindful that through patient suffering, we learn to rely on you more. Amen.

Day 4

When we speak of serving God, we often imagine that whatever we direct toward God must be in some mystical sense through prayer or meditation. However, in the Bible, we are told that God is loved and hated when we love and hate our neighbor in turn. To serve our neighbor is to serve God. But the opposite is also true. If we despise our neighbor, it is as if we despise God himself.

Meditations from St. Catherine

I wish also that you should know that every virtue is obtained by means of your neighbor, and likewise, every defect; he, therefore, who stands in hatred of Me, does an injury to his neighbor, and to himself, who is his own chief neighbor, and this injury is both general and particular. It is general because you are obliged to love your neighbor as yourself, and loving him, you ought to help him spiritually, with prayer, counseling him with words, and assisting him both spiritually and temporally, according to the need in which he may be, at least with your goodwill if you have nothing else. A man therefore, who does not love, does not help him, and thereby does himself an injury; for he cuts off from himself grace, and injures his neighbor, by depriving him of the benefit of the prayers and of the sweet desires that he is bound to offer for him to Me. Thus, every act of help that he performs should proceed from the charity which he has through love of Me. And every evil also, is done by means of his neighbor, for, if he do not love Me, he cannot be in charity with his neighbor; and thus, all evils derive from the soul's deprivation of love of Me and her neighbor; whence, inasmuch as such a man does no good, it follows that he must do evil. To whom does he evil? First of all to himself, and then to his neighbor, not against Me, for no evil can touch Me, except in so far as I count done to Me that which he does to himself. To himself he does the injury of sin, which deprives him of grace, and worse than this he cannot do to his neighbor. Him he injures in not paying him the debt, which he owes him, of love, with which he ought to help him by means of prayer and holy desire offered to Me for him.

A Treatise of Divine Providence

Additional Biblical Reflections: Leviticus 19:18; Matthew 25:31-46; Mark 12:31-31.

PRAYER

Lord, you have said that you will be with us forever. So, too, did you declare that the poor would always be with us. Let us love you through our love of the needy. Let us refrain from doing evil against our fellows lest we do evil to you. In all these things, let us serve you as we serve one another. Amen.

DAY 5

St. Catherine teaches us, following Jesus's own words, that suffering produces patience and refines our faith. She also teaches that our present suffering serves to magnify the fruit and reward of supernatural glory, the promise of Christ that a better future is in store. Thus, we can bear our sufferings patiently, knowing they are temporary. God has a better future planned for us.

MEDITATIONS FROM ST. CATHERINE

Dearest brother in Christ Jesus: I Catherine, a useless servant, comfort and bless thee and invite thee to a sweet and most holy patience, for without patience we could not please God. So I beg you, in order that you may receive the fruit of your tribulations, that you assume the armor of patience. And should it seem very hard to you to endure your many troubles, bear in memory three things, that you may endure more patiently. First, I want you to think of the shortness of your time, for on one day you are not certain of the morrow. We may truly say that we do not feel past trouble, nor that which is to come, but only the moment of time at which we are. Surely, then, we ought to endure patiently, since the time is so short. The second thing is, for you to consider the fruit which follows our troubles. For St. Paul says there is no comparison between our troubles and the fruit and reward of supernal glory. The third is, for you to consider the loss which results to those who endure in wrath and impatience; for loss follows this here, and eternal punishment to the soul.

To Benincasa Her Brother When He Was in Florence

Additional Biblical Reflections: Romans 8:18-31; 2 Corinthians 4:16; 1 Peter 5:10.

PRAYER

Lord, you have planned an incredible and glorious future for your children. Grant us patience amidst this world's tribulations, knowing that these things are temporary, and the glory you have promised is eternal. In Jesus's name. Amen.

DAY 6

It is easy to remain in our faith when life is going well. However, when bad things befall us, we are forced upon a crossroads—to turn away from God and follow our own path with resentment harbored against Him, or turn to God all the more and trust Him despite the unclear path ahead. In today's meditation, St. Catherine urges us to follow the Lord's path at all times.

MEDITATIONS FROM ST. CATHERINE

Once our sweet Saviour said to a very dear daughter of His, "Dost thou know how those people act who want to fulfil My will in consolation and in sweetness and joy? When they are deprived of these things, they wish to depart from My will, thinking to do well and to avoid offence; but false sensuality lurks in them, and to escape pains it falls into offence without perceiving it. But if the soul were wise and had the light of My will within, it would look to the fruit and not to the sweetness. What is the fruit of the soul? Hatred of itself and love of Me. This hate and love are the issue of self-knowledge; then the soul knows its faulty self to be nothing, and it sees in itself My goodness, which keeps its will good; and it sees what a person I have made it, in order that it may serve Me in greater perfection, and judges that I have made it for the best, and for its own greatest good. Such a man as this, dearest daughter, does not wish for time to suit himself, because he has learned humility; knowing his infirmity, he does not trust in his own wish, but is faithful to Me. He clothes him in My highest and eternal will, because he sees that I neither give nor take away, save for your sanctification; and he sees that love alone impels Me to give you sweetness and to take it from you. For this cause he cannot grieve over any consolation that might be taken from him within or without, by demon or fellow-creature— because he sees that, were this not for his good, I should not permit it. Therefore this man rejoices because he has light within and without, and is so illumined that when the devil approaches his mind with shadows to confuse him, saying, 'This is for thy sins,' he replies like a person who shrinks not from suffering, saying, 'Thanks be to my Creator, who has remembered me in the time of shadows, punishing me by pain in finite time. Great is this love, which will not punish me in the infinite future.' Oh, what tranquility of mind has this soul, because it has freed itself from the self-will which brings storm! But not thus does he whose self-will is lively within, seeking things after his own way!"

To The Venerable Religious, Brother Antonio of Nizza, of The Order of The Hermit Brothers of Saint Augustine at the Wood of The Lake

Additional Biblical Reflections: Luke 22:42; John 8:11; 2 Peter 2:22.

PRAYER

Lord, your promises are always sure. Let us always remember the future you have set before us in your word so that when life's trials befall us and the Devil deceives us to believe that all things are helpless, we will nonetheless remain steadfast in pursuit of you. Amen.

DAY 7

Today, St. Catherine encourages us to guard against hollow penance or corporal exercises that are done without the affection of the soul. In other words, she cautions against "going through the motions" without a heart that fervently seeks God alongside such action. Prayer, piety, and ritual are fine and good—but if performed merely for the sake of the action without the worshipper's devotion, they merit little.

MEDITATIONS FROM ST. CATHERINE

I wish therefore that the works of penance, and of other corporal exercises, should be observed merely as means, and not as the fundamental affection of the soul. For, if the principal affection of the soul were placed in penance, I should receive a finite thing like a word, which, when it has issued from the mouth, is no more, unless it has issued with affection of the soul, which conceives and brings forth virtue in truth; that is, unless the finite operation, which I have called a word, should be joined with the affection or love, in which case it would be grateful and pleasant to Me. And this is because such a work would not be alone, but accompanied by true discretion, using corporal works as means, and not as the principal foundation; for it would not be becoming that that principal foundation should be placed in penance only, or in any exterior corporal act, such works being finite, since they are done in finite time, and also because it is often profitable that the creature omit them, and even that she be made to do so.

A Treatise of Discretion

Additional Biblical Reflections: Matthew 15:2-6; 2 Thessalonians 3:6; 1 Timothy 1:4.

PRAYER

Lord, you have given us a wealth of tradition and practice that can draw us closer to you if accompanied by affection and devotion. However, ensure, Lord, that we do not misuse these gifts in exercises of vanity but that they might be rightly cherished and revered, with you always at the heart of our prayers and devotions. Amen.

DAY 8

Often, spiritual seekers imagine themselves as merely lost looking for a single path—and there might be many—whereby one might escape their darkness and see some light. However, what St. Catherine reminds us is that sin has done more than left us wandering lost. It has come upon us like a deluge and would drown us if the Lord had not offered His Bridge to rescue us. When in peril, who would reject a single hand that reaches out because it is not the hand one chose for oneself, or it isn't the sort of rescuer one had imagined? Such a person we would rightly deem a fool. Thus, it is not unloving that God should demand that if we hope to be saved, we should take home of Christ alone. It is the height of love, in fact, that He would bid us cling to Him and no other.

MEDITATIONS FROM ST. CATHERINE

"Wherefore I have told you that I have made a Bridge of My Word, of My only-begotten Son, and this is the truth. I wish that you, My children, should know that the road was broken by the sin and disobedience of Adam, in such a way, that no one could arrive at Eternal Life. Wherefore men did not render Me glory in the way in which they ought to have, as they did not participate in that Good for which I had created them, and My truth was not fulfilled. This truth is that I have created man to My own image and similitude, in

order that he might have Eternal Life, and might partake of Me, and taste My supreme and eternal sweetness and goodness. But, after sin had closed Heaven and bolted the doors of mercy, the soul of man produced thorns and prickly brambles, and My creature found in himself rebellion against himself.

"And the flesh immediately began to war against the Spirit, and, losing the state of innocence, became a foul animal, and all created things rebelled against man, whereas they would have been obedient to him, had he remained in the state in which I had placed him. He, not remaining therein, transgressed My obedience, and merited eternal death in soul and body. And, as soon as he had sinned, a tempestuous flood arose, which ever buffets him with its waves, bringing him weariness and trouble from himself, the devil, and the world. Every one was drowned in the flood, because no one, with his own justice alone, could arrive at Eternal Life. And so, wishing to remedy your great evils, I have given you the Bridge of My Son, in order that, passing across the flood, you may not be drowned, which flood is the tempestuous sea of this dark life. See, therefore, under what obligations the creature is to Me, and how ignorant he is, not to take the remedy which I have offered, but to be willing to drown."

A Treatise of Discretion

Additional Biblical Reflections: Deuteronomy 6:4; John 14:6; 1 Timothy 2:5.

PRAYER

Lord, in our desperation, you sent your Son to rescue us from our perilous estate. Thank you, Lord, for your salvation. Let us not be foolishly deceived by false saviors or paths of our own making, but let us always hold fast to your salvation so that we might be drawn from the water and live forever in your image. Amen.

DAY 9

In today's meditation, St. Catherine continues speaking from a revelation from God, according to the metaphor of God's Bridge, Jesus, who is our salvation. Here the full scope of His redemptive plan is in view. He came not merely to save some, but to save all the earth, those who would cling to His bridge and be lifted from the flood of sin.

MEDITATIONS FROM ST. CATHERINE

"Open, my daughter, the eye of your intellect, and you will see the accepted and the ignorant, the imperfect, and also the perfect who follow Me in truth, so that you may grieve over the damnation of the ignorant, and rejoice over the perfection of My beloved servants.

"You will see further how those bear themselves who walk in the light, and those who walk in the darkness. I also wish you to look at the Bridge of My only-begotten Son, and see the greatness thereof, for it reaches from Heaven to earth, that is, that the earth of your humanity is joined to the greatness of the Deity thereby. I say then that this Bridge reaches from Heaven to earth, and constitutes the union which I have made with man.

"This was necessary, in order to reform the road which was broken, as I said

to you, in order that man should pass through the bitterness of the world, and arrive at life; but the Bridge could not be made of earth sufficiently large to span the flood and give you Eternal Life, because the earth of human nature was not sufficient to satisfy for guilt, to remove the stain of Adam's sin. Which stain corrupted the whole human race and gave out a stench, as I have said to you above. It was, therefore, necessary to join human nature with the height of My nature, the Eternal Deity, so that it might be sufficient to satisfy for the whole human race, so that human nature should sustain the punishment, and that the Divine nature, united with the human, should make acceptable the sacrifice of My only Son, offered to Me to take death from you and to give you life.

"So the height of the Divinity, humbled to the earth, and joined with your humanity, made the Bridge and reformed the road. Why was this done? In order that man might come to his true happiness with the angels. And observe, that it is not enough, in order that you should have life, that My Son should have made you this Bridge, unless you walk thereon."

A Treatise of Discretion

Additional Biblical Reflections: Genesis 12:1-9; Luke 19:10; John 3:16-17.

PRAYER

Lord, you have a heart that beats for the whole world, all the creatures you have made. As such, let us readily take hold of your redemption – the great Bridge that your Son has forged – and be saved so that all the world might come to know you. Amen.

DAY 10

The Holy Spirit was sent by the Father and the Son following Christ's ascension, in which He might guide us in the truth and be an ever-present consoler even as our Lord began His reign at the right hand of the Father. Furthermore, should we hope to find Christ, we must pursue Him through the Spirit, the Word through which the Spirit speaks, and through the Sacrament of Christ's Body and Blood.

MEDITATIONS FROM ST. CATHERINE

"When My only-begotten Son returned to Me, forty days after the resurrection, this Bridge, namely Himself, arose from the earth, that is, from among the conversation of men, and ascended into Heaven by virtue of the Divine Nature and sat at the right hand of Me, the Eternal Father, as the angels said, on the day of the Ascension, to the disciples, standing like dead men, their hearts lifted on high, and ascended into Heaven with the wisdom of My Son – 'Do not stand here any longer, for He is seated at the right hand of the Father!' When He, then, had thus ascended on high, and returned to Me the Father, I sent the Master, that is the Holy Spirit, who came to you with My power and the wisdom of My Son, and with His own clemency, which is the essence of the Holy Spirit. He is one thing with Me, the Father, and with My Son. And He built up the road of the doctrine which My Truth had left in the world. Thus,

though the bodily presence of My Son left you, His doctrine remained, and the virtue of the stones founded upon this doctrine, which is the way made for you by this Bridge. For first, He practiced this doctrine and made the road by His actions, giving you His doctrine by example rather than by words; for He practiced, first Himself, what He afterwards taught you, then the clemency of the Holy Spirit made you certain of the doctrine, fortifying the minds of the disciples to confess the truth, and to announce this road, that is, the doctrine of Christ crucified, reproving, by this means, the world of its injustice and false judgment, of which injustice and false judgment, I will in time discourse to you at greater length."

A Treatise of Discretion

Additional Biblical Reflections: Genesis 1:1-2; John 14:26; 16:27; Acts 2.

PRAYER

Lord, you did not abandon us when you ascended into Heaven but sent your Spirit that you might be with us, no matter from whence we hail, and guide us in your truth until your final return. Preserve us through your Spirit so that we might not waiver from your doctrine until all truth is revealed in the coming of your Son. Amen.

DAY 11

In today's meditation, St. Catherine discerns between three different kinds of prayer: perpetual, verbal, and mental. Perpetually, we maintain a sort of connection with God on a spiritual level, like an open channel between ourselves and God, constantly open to His voice and guidance. Then, we learn to pray verbally—but this is not about merely verbalizing words. Verbal prayer is meant to arrest the mind with holy desire. Thus, it is not sufficient to simply speak words while the mind wanders. Rather, the mind must take hold of the words of prayer so that the whole person is united to God.

MEDITATIONS FROM ST. CATHERINE

Prayer is of three sorts. The one is perpetual: it is the holy perpetual desire, which prays in the sight of God, whatever thou art doing; for this desire directs all thy works, spiritual and corporal, to His honour, and therefore it is called perpetual. Of this it seems that Saint Paul the glorious was talking when he said: Pray without ceasing.

The other kind is vocal prayer, when the offices or other prayers are said aloud. This is ordained to reach the third— that is, mental prayer: your soul reaches this when it uses vocal prayer in prudence and humility, so that while the tongue speaks the heart is not far from God. But one must exert one's self to hold and establish one's heart in the force of divine charity. And whenever one felt one's mind to be visited by God, so that it was drawn to think of its Creator in any wise, it ought to abandon vocal prayer, and to fix its mind with the force of love upon that wherein it sees God visit it; then, if it has time, when this has ceased, it ought to take up the vocal prayer again, in order that the mind may always stay full and not empty. And although many conflicts of diverse kinds should abound in prayer, and darkness of mind with much confusion, the devil making the soul feel that her prayer was not pleasing to God— nevertheless, she ought not to give up on account of those conflicts and shadows, but to abide firm in fortitude and long perseverance, considering that the devil so does to draw her away from prayer the mother, and God permits it to test the fortitude and constancy of that soul. Also, in order that by those conflicts and shadows she may know herself not to be, and in the goodwill which she feels preserved within her may know the goodness of God, Who is Giver and Preserver of good and holy wills: such wills as are not vouchsafed to all who want them.

By this means she attains to the third and last— mental prayer, in which she receives the reward for the labours she underwent in her imperfect vocal prayer. Then she tastes the milk of faithful prayer. She rises above herself— that is, above the gross impulses of the senses— and with angelic mind unites herself with God by force of love, and sees and knows with the light of thought, and clothes herself with truth. She is made the sister of angels; she abides with her Bridegroom on the table of crucified desire, rejoicing to seek the honour of God and the salvation of souls; since well she sees that for this the Eternal Bridegroom ran to the shameful death of the Cross, and thus fulfilled obedience to the Father, and our salvation.

To Sister Eugenia, Her Niece at the Convent of Saint Agnes

Additional Biblical Reflections: Psalm 102; Matthew 6:16-18; 1 Thessalonians 5:17.

PRAYER

Lord, envelop our lives in prayer. Let us maintain perpetual prayer, constantly aligned with your word and will. Grant that the words we pray not be said in vain, but that by arresting our hearts and minds, our prayers might rise to you like sweet incense. Grant these requests, Lord, so that we might live according to your will.

DAY 12

Writing at a time when it was common amongst monastics to engage in self-flagellation, follow extreme fasts, and other methods meant to mortify the flesh, St. Catherine warns that the body is not itself the seat of sin, but the self-will that operates through the flesh. Whatever spiritual discipline we engage, we must not lose the forest for the trees. Sin is not a flaw in the body—God created the body and declared it good. The sinful "flesh," rather, is as such because of the inward focus of the will.

MEDITATIONS FROM ST. CATHERINE

The soul must not stay content because it has arrived at gaining the general light; nay, it ought to go on with all zeal to the perfect light. For since men are at first imperfect rather than perfect, they should advance in light to perfection. Two kinds of perfect people walk in this perfect light. There are some who give themselves to castigating their body perfectly, doing very great harsh penance; and that the flesh may not rebel against the reason, they have placed all their desire rather on mortifying their body than on slaying their self-will. These people feed at the table of penitence and are good and perfect; but unless they have a great humility and conform themselves not wholly to judge according to the will of God and not according to that of men, they often wrong their perfection, making themselves judges of those who do not walk in the same way in which they do. This happens to them because they have put more thought and desire on mortifying their body than on slaying their self-will.

To Brother William of England of the Hermit Brothers of St. Augustine

Additional Biblical Reflections: Luke 12:22-23; Romans 7:12-25; 1 Corinthians 6:13-20; 9:25-27.

PRAYER

Lord, you created us in the body and declared our bodies good. Let us not abuse our bodies, neither let us be overindulgent in the pleasures of the flesh. Rather, let our disciplines and pieties conform our will to you so that we will not desire what pleases ourselves but only and always what pleases you. Amen.

DAY 13

It is easy to miss the forest for the trees. Often in our efforts toward piety, we lose the heart of it—the pursuit of God—for the sake of self-serving disciplines. Furthermore, in our effort to enjoy the life God has given us, we are prone to self-indulgence. Today's meditation picks up on the theme of moderation—to discipline the flesh, but not abuse it. To enjoy God's gifts but not link one's passions to worldly things, Christ must remain at the center of all we do.

MEDITATIONS FROM ST. CATHERINE

Be a dispenser to the poor of your temporal substance. Submit you to the yoke of holy and true obedience. Kill, kill your own will, that it may not be so tied to your relatives, and mortify your body, and do not so pamper it in delicate ways. Despise yourself, and have in regard neither rank nor riches, for virtue is the only thing that makes us gentlefolk, and the riches of this life are the worst of poverty when possessed with inordinate love apart from God. Recall to memory what the glorious Jerome said about this, which one can never repeat often enough, forbidding that widows should abound in daintiness, or keep their face anointed, or their garments choice or delicate. Nor should their conversation be with vain or dissolute young women, but in the cell: they should do like the turtle- dove, who, when her companion has died, mourns forever, and keeps to herself, and wants no other company. Limit your intercourse, dearest and most beloved Sister, to Christ crucified; set your affection and desire on following Him by the way of shame and true humility, in gentleness, binding you to the Lamb with the bands of charity. This my soul desires, that you may be a true daughter, and a bride consecrated to Christ, and a fruitful field, not sterile, but full of the sweet fruits of true virtues. Hasten, hasten, for time is short and the road is long. And if you gave all you have in the world, time would not pause for you from running its course. I say no more. Remain in the holy and sweet grace of God.

To Monna Colomba in Lucca

Additional Biblical Reflections: Deuteronomy 14:12; Romans 8:30-39; 1 Corinthians 10:31.

PRAYER

Lord, it is easy to be distracted by the things of this world. So, too, can we be distracted from you by blindly pursuing the very practices that ought to drive us toward you more fervently. May your Son always be at the heart of our faith and His light always in our eyes so that we might see clearly and not be blinded by the passions of this flesh and world. Amen.

DAY 14

It has been said that while the Devil is a lion, he is a lion on a leash, the length of which is determined by God. Today, St. Catherine reminds us that even the Devil—like how God once used ungodly Babylon as his instrument to discipline Israel—is His instrument of justice, and when he attacks, we might prove ourselves virtuous and faithful.

MEDITATIONS FROM ST. CATHERINE

The Devil, dearest daughter, is the instrument of My Justice to torment the souls who have miserably offended Me. And I have set him in this life to tempt and molest My creatures, not for My creatures to be conquered, but that they may conquer, proving their virtue, and receive from Me the glory of victory. And no one should fear any battle or temptation of the Devil that may come to him, because I have made My creatures strong, and have given them strength of will, fortified in the Blood of my Son, which will, neither Devil nor creature can move, because it is yours, given by Me. You therefore, with free arbitration, can hold it or leave it, according as you please. It is an arm, which, if you place it in the hands of the Devil, straightway becomes a knife, with which he strikes you and slays you. But if man do not give this knife of his will into the hands of the Devil, that is, if he do not consent to his temptations and molestations, he will never be injured by the guilt of sin in any temptation, but will even be fortified by it, when the eye of his intellect is opened to see My love which allowed him to be tempted, so as to arrive at virtue, by being proved. For one does not arrive at virtue except through knowledge of self, and knowledge of Me, which knowledge is more perfectly acquired in the time of temptation, because then man knows himself to be nothing, being unable to lift off himself the pains and vexations which he would flee; and he knows Me in his will, which is fortified by My goodness, so that it does not yield to these thoughts.

A Treatise of Discretion

Additional Biblical Reflections: Jeremiah 51:20-25; Job 1:6-12; 1 Peter 4:12-13.

PRAYER

Lord, we need not fear the Devil for he is but an instrument in your hand whose threats can extend no further than you permit. Grant us steadfastness when afflicted by the foe so that we will not be destroyed but refined in the faith and endure unto life everlasting. Amen.

DAY 15

Amid temptation—be it from the Devil or the flesh—St. Catherine reminds us that Christ is still present. His presence, His truth, abides with us, giving us the strength to extinguish the fiery darts of the foe. Of course, we do not always *feel* His presence beside us. Here, St. Catherine simply bids us consider the will. If we desire that the Lord be with us, we can be certain He is, regardless of whether we feel His presence, for He has promised to be amongst those who desire Him in faith.

MEDITATIONS FROM ST. CATHERINE

I remember that I heard this said once to a servant of God, and it was said to her by the Sweet Primal Truth, when she was abiding in very great pain and temptation, and among other things, felt the greatest confusion, in so much that the devil said: "What wilt thou do? for all the time of thy life thou shalt abide in these pains, and then thou shalt have hell." She then answered with manly heart, and without any fear, and with holy hatred of herself, saying: "I do not avoid pains, for I have chosen pains for my refreshment. And if at the end He should give me hell, I will not therefore abandon serving my Creator. For I am she who am worthy of abiding in hell, because I wronged the Sweet Primal Truth; so, did He give me hell, He would do me no wrong, since I am His." Then our Saviour, in this sweet and true humility, scattered the shadows and torments of the devil, as it happens when the cloud passes that the sun remains; and suddenly came the Presence of Our Saviour. Thence she melted into a river of tears, and said in a sweet glow of love: "O sweet and good Jesus, where wast thou when my soul was in such affliction?" Sweet Jesus, the Spotless Lamb, replied: "I was beside thee. For I move not, and never leave My creature, unless the creature leave Me through mortal sin." And that woman abode in sweet converse with Him, and said: "If Thou wast with me, how did I not feel Thee? How can it be that being by the fire, I should not feel the heat? And I felt nothing but freezing cold, sadness, and bitterness, and seemed to myself full of mortal sins." He replied sweetly, and said: "Dost thou wish Me to show thee, daughter mine, how in those conflicts thou didst not fall into mortal sin, and how I was beside thee? Tell me, what is it that makes sin mortal? Only the will. For sin and virtue consist in the consent of the will; there is no sin nor virtue, unless voluntarily wrought. This will was not in thee; for had it been, thou wouldst have taken joy and delight in the suggestions of the devil; but since the will was not there, thou didst grieve over them, and suffer for fear of doing wrong. So thou seest that sin and virtue consist in choice— wherefore I tell thee that thou shouldst not, on account of these conflicts, fall into disordered confusion.

To Sister Bartolomea Della Seta Nun in the Convent of Santo Stefano At Pisa

Additional Biblical Reflections: Exodus 33:14; Psalm 140:13; Matthew 28:18-20.

PRAYER

Lord, your presence is not contingent on a feeling or our circumstances. You promised that you would be with us and, therefore, we can be sure that so long as we desire it, you will be with us come what may. Let this truth be ever before us and that we might not lose hope amid hardship. Amen.

DAY 16

Fear can be one of the most controlling and paralyzing forces in life. Some fears are rational, and others do not make much sense, but they can be paralyzing no less. Regardless, we all know fear. However, fear can be dangerous. It can lead to sin. It also stems from doubt rather than faith. Today, St. Catherine reminds us that we have nothing to fear in Christ and that we can put on the armor of God and face all of our fears.

MEDITATIONS FROM ST. CATHERINE

And I tell you on behalf of Christ crucified, most sweet and holy father, not to fear for any reason whatsoever. Come in security: trust you in Christ sweet Jesus: for, doing what you ought, God will be above you, and there will be no one who shall be against you. Up, father, like a man! For I tell you that you have no need to fear. You ought to come; come, then. Come gently, without any fear. And if any at home wish to hinder you, say to them bravely, as Christ said when St. Peter, through tenderness, wished to draw Him back from going to His passion; Christ turned to him, saying, "Get thee behind Me, Satan; thou art an offence to Me, seeking the things which are of men, and not those which are of God. Wilt thou not that I fulfil the will of My Father?" Do you likewise, sweetest father, following Him as His vicar, deliberating and deciding by yourself, and saying to those who would hinder you, "If my life should be spent a thousand times, I wish to fulfil the will of my Father." Although bodily life be laid down for it, yet seize on the life of grace and the means of winning it forever. Now comfort you and fear not, for you have no need. Put on the armour of the most holy Cross, which is the safety and the life of Christians. Let talk who will, and hold you firm in your holy resolution.

To Gregory XI

Additional Biblical Reflections: Isaiah 41:10; 2 Timothy 1:7; 1 John 4:18.

PRAYER

Lord, you are the source of our courage. When faced with the burden of the world's sin and the curse of the cross, you had no fear but stepped forward toward Golgotha with unwavering resolve. Let us follow your example and know that there is nothing to fear, for you have conquered all threats and emerged again in victory. Amen.

DAY 17

It is easy to grow weary in this life, particularly when our efforts do not seem to bear fruit. This can also be our experience with faith. No matter how many times we attend mass, how many sermons we hear, how many prayers we pray, we often find ourselves stagnant without any real spiritual growth. Today, St. Catherine reminds us to persevere in virtue—for perseverance is what stands between fortitude and patience and prevents us from falling into sin.

MEDITATIONS FROM ST. CATHERINE

Dearest brother in Christ sweet Jesus: I Catherine, servant and slave of the servants of Jesus Christ, write to you in His precious Blood, with desire to see you constant and persevering in virtue; for it is not he who begins who is crowned, but only he who perseveres. For Perseverance is the Queen who is crowned; she stands between Fortitude and true Patience, but she alone receives a crown of glory. So I want you, dearest brother, to be constant and persevering in virtue, that you may receive the reward of your every labour. I hope in the great goodness of God that He will fortify you in such wise that neither demon nor fellow-creature can make you look back to your vomit.

To Messer Ristoro Canigiani

Additional Biblical Reflections: Matthew 24:13; James 1:2-12; Hebrews 12:1-15.

Prayer

Lord, give us a spirit of perseverance to face all hardship, all temptation, and all doubt without wavering from the course of faith that you have set before us. Grant us an unwavering commitment to your path so that we might not fall into sin but endure and receive your crown of glory. Amen.

DAY 18

It is easy to pray for those whom we love. We can even manage to pray for acquaintances, magistrates, and presidents we do not know personally. Praying for our enemies, for those who conspire against us, is another thing altogether. Yet, as Jesus tells us, and St. Catherine reminds us, if we wish our hearts to beat after our Lord's, we must also love and pray for our enemies as well as our friends.

MEDITATIONS FROM ST. CATHERINE

You seem, according to what you write me, to have made a good beginning, in which I rejoice greatly for your salvation, seeing your holy desire. First, you say that you have forgiven every man who had wronged you or wished to wrong you. This is a thing which is very necessary, if you wish to have God in your soul through grace, and to be at rest even according to the world. For he who abides in hate is deprived of God and is in a state of condemnation, and has in this life the foretaste of hell; for he is always gnawing at himself, and hungers for vengeance, and abides in fear. Believing to slay his enemy, he has first killed himself, for he has slain his soul with the knife of hate. Such men as these, who think to slay their enemy, slay themselves. He who truly forgives through the love of Christ crucified, has peace and quiet, and suffers no perturbation; for the wrath that perturbs is slain in his soul, and God the Rewarder of every good gives him His grace and at the last eternal life. What joy the soul, then, receives, and gladness and rest in its conscience, the tongue could never tell. And even according to the world, very great honour is given to the man who through love of virtue and magnanimity does not greedily desire to wreak vengeance on his enemy. So I summon you and comfort you, to persevere in this holy resolution.

To Messer Ristoro Canigiani

Additional Biblical Reflections: Leviticus 19:18; Proverbs 25:21-22; Matthew 5:43-48.

PRAYER

Lord, despite how the world rejected you, you came to embrace the world and redeem it. Let us exhibit this in our lives and love even those who despise us or who would do us harm so that we might draw nearer to you and follow the past of your cross. Amen.

DAY 19

The Lord works through men and women in various ways. Whether through the call of prophets, apostles, or simple worshippers, He nonetheless desires that all come to manifest His will, truth, and presence in the world by embracing holy virtue and resting in grace. Thus, we are all called to seek the Lord. May he manifest himself through us however He wills.

MEDITATIONS FROM ST. CATHERINE

Do you know how I manifest Myself to the soul who loves Me in truth, and follows the doctrine of My sweet and amorous Word? In many is My virtue manifested in the soul in proportion to her desire, but I make three special manifestations. The first manifestation of My virtue, that is to say, of My love and charity in the soul, is made through the Word of My Son, and shown in the Blood, which He spilled with such fire of love. Now this charity is manifested in two ways; first, in general, to ordinary people, that is to those who live in the ordinary grace of God. It is manifested to them by the many and diverse benefits which they receive from Me. The second mode of manifestation, which is developed from the first, is peculiar to those who have become My friends in the way mentioned above, and is known through a sentiment of the soul, by which they taste, know, prove, and feel it. This second manifestation, however, is in men themselves; they manifesting Me, through the affection of their love.

For though I am no Acceptor of creatures, I am an Acceptor of holy desires, and Myself in the soul in that precise degree of perfection which she seeks in Me. Sometimes I manifest Myself (and this is also a part of the second manifestation) by endowing men with the spirit of prophecy, showing them the things of the future. This I do in many and diverse ways, according as I see need in the soul herself and in other creatures. At other times the third manifestation takes place. I then form in the mind the presence of the Truth, My only-begotten Son, in many ways, according to the will and the desire of the soul. Sometimes she seeks Me in prayer, wishing to know My power, and I satisfy her by causing her to taste and see My virtue. Sometimes she seeks Me in the wisdom of My Son, and I satisfy her by placing His wisdom before the eye of her intellect, sometimes in the clemency of the Holy Spirit and then My Goodness causes her to taste the fire of Divine charity, and to conceive the true and royal virtues, which are founded on the pure love of her neighbor.

A Treatise of Discretion

Additional Biblical Reflections: Isaiah 46:9-10; Ephesians 4:11-32; Hebrews 1:1-14.

PRAYER

Lord, while you never change, you nonetheless manifest your presence for us in many callings and revelations. Give us eyes to see your truth so that we do not fall into sin or vice, but always pursue the path you have lit ahead of us in our pursuit of you, your will, and your holy virtue. Amen.

DAY 20

Not all of us can pray as incessantly as a monk or nun. Such is not everyone's vocation. Nonetheless, what St. Catherine tells us today is of great value, lest even our time in prayer becomes an occasion for the Devil to tempt us, making even our prayers a burden. We have all experienced times when, tired of what seems to be prayer without progress or clear answers from God, we begin exchanging our time set aside for prayer for other tasks. We tell ourselves we will get back to it later—but then forget about it and complete the day without any prayer at all. The key, as St. Catherine describes, is to persevere and pray regardless of what we might have on our agenda, or how tired we might be, or how burdensome prayer might be.

MEDITATIONS FROM ST. CATHERINE

"WHEN the soul has passed through the doctrine of Christ crucified, with true love of virtue and hatred of vice, and has arrived at the house of self-knowledge and entered therein, she remains, with her door barred, in watching and constant prayer, separated entirely from the consolations of the world. Why does she thus shut herself in? She does so from fear, knowing her own imperfections, and also from the desire, which she has, of arriving at pure and generous love. And because she sees and knows well that in no other way

can she arrive thereat, she waits, with a lively faith for My arrival, through increase of grace in her. How is a lively faith to be recognized? By perseverance in virtue, and by the fact that the soul never turns back for anything, whatever it be, nor rises from holy prayer, for any reason except (note well) for obedience or charity's sake. For no other reason ought she to leave off prayer, for, during the time ordained for prayer, the Devil is wont to arrive in the soul, causing much more conflict and trouble than when the soul is not occupied in prayer. This he does in order that holy prayer may become tedious to the soul, tempting her often with these words: 'This prayer avails you nothing, for you need attend to nothing except your vocal prayers.' He acts thus in order that, becoming wearied and confused in mind, she may abandon the exercise of prayer, which is a weapon with which the soul can defend herself from every adversary, if grasped with the hand of love, by the arm of free choice in the light of the Holy Faith."

A Treatise of Prayer

Additional Biblical Reflections: Jeremiah 33:3; John 15:7; Romans 8:26.

PRAYER

Lord, the Devil once came upon you to tempt you during your forty days of prayer in the wilderness. So, too, does he tempt us during our time of prayer, to dissuade us from this holy task. Sustain us with a spirit of perseverance so that we will not be deceived or abandon our prayers but might, in such times, pray more fervently than before, knowing that you are the one who defeats the great tempter on our behalf. In Jesus's name. Amen.

DAY 21

Once again, in today's meditation, St. Catherine, in the form of a vision granted by the Lord, tells us not to remain content with vocal prayer—since many pray with mere words without love—but not to abandon vocal prayer either. By these methods, we are told, we can advance in degrees. A single conversation might not spark intimacy between a man and a woman, but such conversations plant the seeds of love that could, if properly nurtured, sprout in a beautiful blossom of love and intimacy. So, too, in our prayers with God, the words of prayer alone are not so important as the relationship that is nourished as we persist in vocal prayer, and our affections and heart are gradually taken hold of by His presence in holy conversation.

MEDITATIONS FROM ST. CATHERINE

But do not think that the soul receives such ardor and nourishment from prayer, if she pray only vocally, as do many souls whose prayers are rather words than love. Such as these give heed to nothing except to completing Psalms and saying many paternosters. And when they have once completed their appointed tale, they do not appear to think of anything further, but seem to place devout attention and love in merely vocal recitation, which the soul is not required to do, for, in doing only this, she bears but little fruit, which pleases Me but little. But if you ask Me, whether the soul should abandon vocal prayer, since it does not seem to all that they are called to mental prayer, I should reply 'No.' The soul should advance by degrees, and I know well that, just as the soul is at first imperfect and afterwards perfect, so also is it with her prayer. She should nevertheless continue in vocal prayer, while she is yet imperfect, so as not to fall into idleness. But she should not say her vocal prayers without joining them to mental prayer, that is to say, that while she is reciting, she should endeavor to elevate her mind in My love, with the consideration of her own defects and of the Blood of My only-begotten Son, wherein she finds the breadth of My charity and the remission of her sins. And this she should do, so that self-knowledge and the consideration of her own defects should make her recognize My goodness in herself and continue her exercises with true humility. I do not wish defects to be considered in particular, but in general, so that the mind may not be contaminated by the remembrance of particular and hideous sins. But, as I said, I do not wish the soul to consider her sins, either in general or in particular, without also remembering the Blood and the broadness of My mercy, for fear that otherwise she should be brought to confusion. And together with confusion would come the Devil, who has caused it, under color of contrition and displeasure of sin, and so she would arrive at eternal damnation, not only on account of her confusion, but also through the despair which would come to her, because she did not seize the arm of My mercy. This is one of the subtle devices with which the Devil deludes My servants, and, in order to escape from his deceit, and to be pleasing to Me, you must enlarge your hearts and affections in My boundless mercy, with true humility.

A Treatise of Prayer

Additional Biblical Reflections: Jeremiah 29:12; Matthew 6:5-8; Luke 11:9; Colossians 4:2.

PRAYER

Lord, let us neither be content with praying in words alone nor let us grow weary of such prayers that we imagine they are fruitless. For you have commanded us to pray not to please you by obedience alone, but that through our obedience to prayer, bathe us in your love. Amen.

DAY 22

In today's meditation, St. Catherine, again in a rapturous vision, describes the conversion of St. Paul—undoubtedly the most remarkable and one of the most dramatic conversions in the Bible—from God's perspective. We hear how it was Christ crucified alone who affected such a radical change in the former Pharisee. In Christ crucified, St. Paul saw the image of dying as self-perfect contrition—and there also he found the strength to take up His cross and endure pains for the sake of the very Lord whom he had persecuted before. There is no instrument more effective in converting the godless to the godly than the truth of Christ crucified—for the radical change from death to life can affect each of us, no matter how far into mortal sin we have fallen, and restore us in His image.

MEDITATIONS FROM ST. CATHERINE

"Paul, then, had seen and tasted this good, when I drew him up into the third heaven, that is into the height of the Trinity, where he tasted and knew My Truth, receiving fully the Holy Spirit, and learning the doctrine of My Truth, the Word Incarnate. The soul of Paul was clothed, through feeling and union, in Me, Eternal Father, like the blessed ones in Eternal Life, except that his soul was not separated from his body, except through this feeling and union. But it being pleasing to My Goodness to make of him a vessel of election in the

abyss of Me, Eternal Trinity, I dispossessed him of Myself, because on Me can no pain fall, and I wished him to suffer for My name; therefore I placed before him, as an object for the eyes of his intellect, Christ crucified, clothing him with the garment of His doctrine, binding and fettering him with the clemency of the Holy Spirit and inflaming him with the fire of charity. He became a vessel, disposed and reformed by My Goodness, and, on being struck, made no resistance, but said: 'My Lord, what do You wish me to do? Show me that which it is Your pleasure for me to do, and I will do it.' Which I answered when I placed before him Christ crucified, clothing him with the doctrine of My charity. I illuminated him perfectly with the light of true contrition, by which he extirpated his defects, and founded him in My charity."

A Treatise of Prayer

Additional Biblical Reflections: Acts 9:1-19; 1 Corinthians 1:23-24; Galatians 1:11-24.

PRAYER

Lord, you once turned a persecutor into an apostle to the nations. Let us ever be mindful of Christ crucified so that you will turn us from our wayward path and various forms of disobedience and restore us to be used as the instruments of your will. Amen.

DAY 23

In today's meditation, St. Catherine describes a mature posture of faith. This posture sees a brother or sister who excels in holiness, and, in doing so—rather than despising them for exceeding one's piety—one develops a "holy envy," which emulates the other, finding their pious brother or sister inspiring, and thus not begrudging them not at all. When one who is mature in the faith sees one of a lesser estate—someone poor or lacking in holiness—they do not imagine themselves greater than the other but rather does as our Lord does and embraces the poor, dining with them in a holy fellowship. We see here a pattern whereby the Lord uses us to help one another excel in holiness. Casting aside all pretenses of pride, jealousy, or status, we embrace one another and are thankful for what the Lord has ordained in each of our present estates in His desire to bring us all, together, toward Him in greater holiness and obedience.

MEDITATIONS FROM ST. CATHERINE

"The obedient man wishes to be the first to enter choir and the last to leave it, and when he sees a brother more obedient than himself he regards him in his eagerness with a holy envy, stealing from him the virtue in which he excels, not wishing, however, that his brother should have less thereof, for if he wished this he would be separated from brotherly love. The obedient man does not leave the

refectory, but visits it continually and delights at being at table with the poor. And as a sign that he delights therein, and so as to have no reason to remain without, he has abandoned his temporal substance, observing so perfectly the vow of poverty that he blames himself for considering even the necessities of his body. His cell is full of the odor of poverty, and not of clothes; he has no fear that thieves will come to rob him, or that rust or moths will corrupt his garments; and if anything is given to him, he does not think of laying it by for his own use, but freely shares it with his brethren, not thinking of the morrow, but rather depriving himself today of what he needs, thinking only of the kingdom of heaven and how he may best observe true obedience."

Treatise of Obedience

Additional Biblical Reflections: John 8:39; Hebrews 13:7; 2 Thessalonians 3:7-9

PRAYER

Lord, let us not consider ourselves greater or lesser than our fellows but, rather, help us to see them as a gift from you—either that we might emulate our brothers and sisters in their greater obedience or cherish our impoverished believers and embrace them in the opportunity to demonstrate your charity. We pray that through all these things, your body will be built up in love and in the image of Christ crucified, rather than perplexed by human pride and jealousy. In Jesus's name. Amen.

DAY 24

Today, St. Catherine ponders the proper attitude we must have when receiving the Eucharist or Holy Communion. By it, we are led to contemplate the mystery of our Lord's holy incarnation and, alongside it, brought to holy contemplation on our need for the Sacrament through meditation on our sins and faults—the very sins Christ atones for through His holy sacrifice.

MEDITATIONS FROM ST. CATHERINE

We have seen that we must seek the kingdom of Heaven prudently: now I answer you about the attitude we should hold toward the Holy Communion, and how it befits us to take it. We should not use a foolish humility, as do secular men of the world. I say, it befits us to receive that sweet Sacrament, because it is the food of souls without which we cannot live in grace. Therefore no bond is so great that it cannot and must not be broken, that we may come to this sweet Sacrament. A man must do on his part as much as he can, and that is enough. How ought we to receive it? With the light of most holy faith, and with the mouth of holy desire. In the light of faith you shall contemplate all God and all Man in that Host. Then the impulse that follows the intellectual perception, receives with tender love and holy meditation on its sins and faults, whence it arrives at contrition, and considers the generosity of the immeasurable love of

God, who in so great love has given Himself for our food. Because one does not seem to have that perfect contrition and disposition which he himself would wish, he must not therefore turn away; for goodwill alone is sufficient, and the disposition which on his part exists.

To Messer Ristoro Canigiani

Additional Biblical Reflections: Mark 14:22-25; John 6:51; 1 Corinthians 10:16-17.

PRAYER

Lord, you have given us the blessed Sacrament of your body and blood so that we might truly feast on you, for you are the nourishment of both body and soul, and through our encounter with your presence, we might be more aware of our need of you and your desire for us. Grant us a holy desire for your Sacrament so that we might be nourished in the faith unto life everlasting. In Jesus's name. Amen.

DAY 25

It is a wondrous thing of our faith that the youngest child can take hold of it, and aged theologians still contemplate its truths. Today, St. Catherine reminds us that knowledge is the foundation of it all—the goodness and love of God, the law of God, which reveals our sin, and an awareness of our wretchedness. With this knowledge at the forefront of our minds, we know all we need to take hold of Christ and advance our knowledge of the faith.

MEDITATIONS FROM ST. CATHERINE

What do we need to know? The great goodness of God, and His unspeakable love toward us; the perverse law which always fights against the Spirit, and our own wretchedness. In this knowledge the soul begins to render His due to God; that is, glory and praise to His Name, loving Him above everything, and the neighbour as one's self, with eager desire for virtue; and the soul bestows hate and displeasure on itself, hating in itself vice, and its own sensuousness, which is the cause of every vice. The soul wins all virtue and grace in the knowledge of itself, abiding therein with light, as was said. Where shall the soul find the wealth of contrition for its sins, and the abundance of God's mercy? In this House of Self-Knowledge.

To Messer Ristoro Canigiani

Additional Biblical Reflections: Exodus 20:1-26; Romans 7:1-25; 1 John 2:1-29.

PRAYER

Lord, you have given us your law not that your demands might burn us but that we might become more aware of our need for you and your mercies. Grant us sufficient knowledge so that we might seek you more and grow in more knowledge of you and, even more, in greater obedience to your perfect will. Amen.

DAY 26

The Lord is no miser. Everything we have in this world and everything He has promised us in the world to come is given us by His gracious heart. Today, St. Catherine reminds us that all His gifts come from His character. She exhorts us to ask the Lord and not withhold our requests because out of His great love, He desires to bless we who seek Him aright with abundance.

MEDITATIONS FROM ST. CATHERINE

You know that God is supremely good, and loved us before we were: and is Eternal Wisdom, and His Power in virtue is immeasurable: so for this reason we are sure that He has power, knowledge, and will to give us what we need. Well we see, in proof, that He gives us more than we know how to ask, and that which was not asked by us. Did we ever ask Him that He should create us reasonable creatures, in His own image and likeness, rather than brute beasts? No. Or that He should create us by Grace by the Blood of the Word, His only-begotten Son, or that He should give us Himself for food, perfect God and perfect Man, flesh and blood, body and soul, united to Deity? Beyond these most high gifts, which are so great, and show such fire of love toward us, that there is no heart so hard that its hardness and coldness would not melt by considering them at all: infinite are the gifts and graces which we receive from Him without asking. Then, since He gives so much without our asking— how much the more will He fulfil our desires when we shall desire a just thing of Him? Nay, who makes us desire and ask it? Only He. Then, if He makes us ask it, it is a sign that He means to fulfil it, and give us what we seek.

To Messer Ristoro Canigiani

Additional Biblical Reflections: Jeremiah 1:5; Matthew 7:71-11; James 4:3.

PRAYER

Lord, you exhibited your abundant generosity from before the time we were made, even when you were determined to speak and thereby created the world and all creatures. Let us learn to ask you for whatever we need in confidence, knowing that you will grant us what we seek whenever we ask in accordance with your will. In Jesus's name. Amen.

DAY 27

Christianity has known many movements focused on charismatic gifts rooted more in feelings than in true effect. In other words, many have mistaken God's genuine presence and gifts for feelings that may or may not be indicative of God's affirmative response to our petitions. Today, St. Catherine reminds us that God sometimes withholds feelings from those who would make more of the feelings than the gift. However, at the same time, He grants deep feelings to others who might require such confirmations of His presence. As always, it is God's intimate knowledge of our hearts that determines, in wisdom, how He chooses to bestow feelings or withhold them.

MEDITATIONS FROM ST. CATHERINE

Sometimes He will do us the grace by giving it to us in effect though not in feeling. He uses this means with foresight, because He knows that if a man felt himself to possess it, either he would slacken the pull of desire, or would fall into presumption; therefore He withdraws the feeling, but not the grace. There are others who both receive and feel, according as it pleases the sweet goodness of our Physician to give to us sick folk; and He gives to everyone in the way that our sickness needs. You see, then, that in any case the yearning of the creature, with which it asks of God, is always fulfilled. Now we see what we ought to seek, and how prudently.

To Messer Ristoro Canigiani

Additional Biblical Reflections: Jeremiah 17:9; Proverbs 28:26; 1 Corinthians 14:33.

PRAYER

Lord, when we ponder your gifts aright, many of us cannot help but be moved with gratitude. Still, it is not the feelings that are the gift; the gift itself is good regardless of our feelings. Grant that we might cherish your gifts, and when such feelings come, let them not become idols unto themselves but an overflow of gratitude for your generosity. Amen.

DAY 28

Today, St. Catherine reminds us how self-love can lead us astray in various ways. Accordingly, she bids us consider the example of Jesus, who was moved not by His love of His glory but rather set His glory aside out of love for us.

MEDITATIONS FROM ST. CATHERINE

So you see, dearest brothers and lords, that self-love ruins the city of the soul, and ruins and overturns the cities of earth. I will that you know that nothing has so divided the world into every kind of people as self-love, from which injustice is forever born. Apparently, dearest brothers, you have a desire to increase and preserve the welfare of your city; and this desire moved you to write to me, poor wretch that I am, full of faults. I heard and saw that letter with tender love, and with wish to satisfy your desires, and to exert me, with what grace God shall give me, to offer you and your city before God with continual prayer. If you shall be just men, and carry on your government as I said above, not in passion nor for self-love or your private good, but for the universal good founded on the Rock Christ sweet Jesus, and if you do all your works in His fear, then by means of prayer you shall preserve the state, the peace and unity of your city. Therefore I beg you by the love of Christ crucified— for there is no other way— that since you have the help of the prayers of the servants of God, you should not fail on your side in what is needful. For did you fail you might to be sure be helped a little by the prayers, but not so much that it would not soon come to nothing; because you ought to help, on your part, to bear this weight.

To the Anziani and Consuls and Gonfalonieri of Blogna

Additional Biblical Reflections: 2 Chronicles 7:14; Mark 10:45; Philippians 2:5-11.

PRAYER

Lord, your word has revealed that pride cometh before the fall. Spare us from self-love and let us learn, instead, from the example of you, who in humility came to us even as a child in a manger, ate with sinners, and died alongside criminals. Grant that we might follow your path of humility so that all we do and say reflects your righteous path glorified before the world. Amen.

DAY 29

Today, St. Catherine reminds us that the Sacrament itself leaves, even after the accidents of bread and wine are consumed, an indelible grace that sustains us in the world. Knowing that we are creatures with five senses, the Lord chooses to engage our human senses through the sacraments so that His graces would not be mere ideas but tangible, tasted on the tongue, and thereby confirmed by His promise.

MEDITATIONS FROM ST. CATHERINE

"See, dearest daughter, in what an excellent state is the soul who receives, as she should, this Bread of Life, this Food of the Angels. By receiving this Sacrament she dwells in Me and I in her, as the fish in the sea, and the sea in the fish -- thus do I dwell in the soul, and the soul in Me -- the Sea Pacific. In that soul grace dwells, for, since she has received this Bread of Life in a state of grace, My grace remains in her, after the accidents of bread have been consumed. I leave you the imprint of grace, as does a seal, which, when lifted from the hot wax upon which it has been impressed, leaves behind its imprint, so the virtue of this Sacrament remains in the soul, that is to say, the heat of My Divine charity, and the clemency of the Holy Spirit. There also remains to you the wisdom of My only-begotten Son, by which the eye of your intellect has been illuminated to see and to know the doctrine of My Truth, and, together with

this wisdom, you participate in My strength and power, which strengthen the soul against her sensual self-love, against the Devil, and against the world. You see then that the imprint remains, when the seal has been taken away, that is, when the material accidents of the bread, having been consumed, this True Sun has returned to Its Center, not that it was ever really separated from It, but constantly united to Me. The Abyss of My loving desire for your salvation has given you, through My dispensation and Divine Providence, coming to the help of your needs, the sweet Truth as Food in this life, where you are pilgrims and travelers, so that you may have refreshment, and not forget the benefit of the Blood. See then how straitly you are constrained and obliged to render Me love, because I love you so much, and, being the Supreme and Eternal Goodness, deserve your love."

A Treatise of Prayer

Additional Biblical Reflections: Exodus 12:21-18; Matthew 4:4; 1 John 1:1-10.

PRAYER

Lord, you have given us true signs of your grace so that we might take hold of you in our earthly estate and thereby ascend to you in the heavens through faith and obedience. Grant that we might avail ourselves of all your gifts and lack none of them, so we can endure in an abundance of grace throughout our lives. Amen.

DAY 30

In today's meditation, St. Catherine reminds us not to judge our fellows. We live in a world where, with little understanding, many are ready and eager to pronounce judgments on others. However, this is a grave error, one that presumes we are equal to God just as the serpent first tempted Adam and Eve that they, too, might know good and evil and play the role of judge. Instead, St. Catherine tells us that we should rest in God's grace and mercy and recognize that God wishes to bestow the same on those whom we would judge. In the end, His justice will prevail—but we are not the executors of His justice; we are the recipients of His mercy and grace.

MEDITATIONS FROM ST. CATHERINE

From living faith one will derive a will in accord with that of God, and will quench in heart and mind the human instinct of judging. The will of God alone shall judge, which seeks and wills naught but our sanctification. In this wise one is not shocked at his neighbour and does not criticize him. Nor does he pass judgment on a man who talks against him: he condemns himself alone, seeing that it is the will of God which permits such men to vex him for his good. Ah, how blessed is the soul which clothes itself in a judgment so gentle! He does not condemn the servants of this world who do him injury; nor does he condemn the servants of God, wishing to drive them in his own way, as many presumptuous, proud men do, who under cloak of the honour of God and the salvation of souls, are shocked by the servants of God, and assume a critical attitude under cover of this cloak, saying: "Such words do not please me." And so a man becomes disturbed in himself, and also makes others disturbed with his tongue, claiming that he speaks through the force of love— and so he thinks he does. But if he will open his eyes, he will find the serpent of presumption under a false aspect, which plays the judge, judging in its own fashion, and not according to the mysteries and the holy and diverse ways in which God works with His creatures. Let human pride be ashamed, and consent to see that in the House of the Eternal Father are many mansions. Let it not seek to impose a rule upon the Holy Spirit: for He is the Rule itself, Giver of the Rule: nor let it measure Him who cannot be measured. The true servant of God, arrayed in His highest eternal will, will not do thus; nay, he will hold in reverence the ways and deeds and habits of God's servants, since he judges them fixed not by man, but by God. For, just because things are not pleasing to us and do not go according to our habits, we ought to be predisposed to believe that they are pleasing to God. We ought not to judge anything at all, nor can we, except what is manifest and open sin. And even this the soul enamoured of God and lost to itself does not assume to judge, except in displeasure for the sin and wrong done to God; and with great compassion for the soul of him who sins, eagerly willing to give itself to any torture for the salvation of that soul.

To Sano Di Maco and all her Other Sons in Siena

Additional Biblical Reflections: Matthew 7:1-5; Romans 14:1-23; 1 Corinthians 4:1-5.

PRAYER

Lord, let us not again commit the original sin that we would see ourselves become like God by judging others. Instead, let us only do what you command: To love one another while reserving judgment to you. For you know the hearts of all people, and we see only the outward works of one's hands. Grant us humble hearts, Lord, that recognize if we were subject to the judgments of men, we, too, would be condemned. Rather, let us rest in your mercy, who judges rightly and redeems abundantly. In Jesus's name. Amen.